154 Cates Poetic "Jim's"

154 Cates Poetic "Jim's"

Jim Cates

Published by Jim Cates

Designed and formatted by
Cozzen Publications
Claremont, NC 28610

First Printing: 2014

ISBN 10: 0982719373
ISBN 13: 978-0-9837193-7-3

Published by Jim Cates 159 Saint Mary's Church Road
Morganton, NC 28655

Printed in the U.S.A

Dedicated to my wife of 52
years,
Georgia Cates.

Ode to Follicular Lymphoma

(1)

I can't believe that old healthy me,

would see a day when chemotherapy

would occur for me.

But alas, it has come to be.

Obviously, I am not over-wrought with glee.

Six hours one day, four the next, I will endure

those injections designed to make me pure.

Six months, every three weeks,

I will repeat the same ordeal.

The goal, of course, is to heal.

(2)

Hallelujah! My platelets are 78,

so my treatments are at the starting gate.

Once again, I begin

the treatments to put me on the mend.

So, for five months or so,

I am back on the go.

Family, friends, and neighbors will be glad

to hear it,

and it sure will boost my spirit.

(3)

Treatment number three is on tap,

during which I probably will have a nice nap.

Of course, my platelets need to cooperate

to be able to keep this date.

Theoretically, this one will put me half-way through,

If not, I sure will be blue.

(4)

Platelets were okay, so,

I got to stay.

Six and a half hours the sera dripped,

any longer and I would have flipped.

After tomorrow,

I wait 26 days for the fourth time again,

then wait 26 more days for number five to begin.

Supposedly, six treatments will do the trick,

and I should be feeling pretty slick.

(5)

I am here for treatment number four,

which is something I have learned NOT to abhor.

Platelets are 106, up from 98,

so, I get to keep my "kemo" date.

Another PET/CT Scan after this treatment to

see how I have fared.

Then, two more to go and hopefully,

further treatments will be spared.

(6)

"Kemo" number five is here,

and this one I hold pretty dear.

Only one more to go,

And then I won't have to shell out so much dough.

Twenty-six days will fly by,

and number six will be welcomed with a

great big sigh.

(7)

J'vais finis!

Today and tomorrow my "kemo" treatments
are to cease.

For the past six months, I have lain here with
no pains,

while watching the life-saving fluids pulse
through my veins.

Now, a check-up every three months to see
if my cure is up to snuff.

I hope so because I have had enough.

(8)

Dr. Thompson, my oncologist, called this morning
to say: "It's time for you to say, "Hooray."

The CT Scan on Tuesday revealed that my spleen
and lymph nodes are in remission,

So with my extra time, I might just take up "fishin"

I believe all those prayers on my behalf
have helped a lot,

and made it unnecessary to use my Saint Mary's
cemetery plot.

So, two more "kemo's" to go,

a total of thirty-three days, and I will be saying a
lot of: "Hip-Hip-Hooray's."

(9)

I'm wondering if I have a poetic bent,

As these verses, I seem compelled to vent.

I jot them down as they occur to me,

If I don't my thoughts will quickly flee.

Six lines I try to make,

Just so I have six -- for heavens sake!

(10)

Sunday morning at church,

for greater understanding we search.

Our Priest (Pastor) presents his/her sermon,

an understanding we must determine.

Next Sunday, we will return,

to hear the Good News for which we all yearn.

(11)

Teaching P.E.

makes me full of glee,

Students run and cavort

and perform athletic things of that sort.

For an hour or so, they run and play,

then, off to study for the rest of the day.

(12)

Sunday morning at church an offering is taken,

so that church expenses can't be forsaken.

A tithe is given by some,

others merely come.

Money is not the only way to contribute,

service to church activities is also an attribute.

(13)

The difference between a Roux and a Slurry,

makes my mind kind of blurry.

I think and think,

but, I only draw a blink (blank).

I hope I get it,

so, I can quit.

(14)

World History, to me,

is a mystery.

We read, read, read

so many students plead.

We answer lots of questions,

after we read the selections.

(15)

Psychology is pretty hard to see,

as we study diligently.

So we can understand how human nature works,

along with all of its quirks.

Sometimes for students, it is pretty tough,

but not for me because I like this stuff.

(16)

A nurse handed a small bottle to me,

and told me to go p......

I did this with no pain,

because I didn't want to incur the nurse's distain.

Perhaps, I have to do this again,

but, of course, with no chagrin.

(17)

To Hickory, once again, we drive,

on time we hope to arrive.

Georgia's radiation time is to be met,

otherwise, a scolding we might get.

Seven weeks daily we make this trek,

It's making both of us a nervous wreck.

(18)

Waffle House for breakfast for Mom and me,

to help us be more healthy.

Everyday we stop and eat,

which, is quite a treat.

A few pounds we will probably add,

which, of course, may make us glad.

(19)

I like to Shag, Shag, Shag, until I drop,

but, sometimes my legs feel like they are going to plop.

I get to sweating quite a bit,

so a malodorous effusion, I sometimes emit.

I hope to keep getting better,

even if I am a "sweat-er."

(20)

Well, I reached my goal,

the Pancake 5k was the tenth race, so I did it,

though at a slower than usual pace.

Two more local races are coming up,

and my goals will be adjusted to win another cup.

That will make number twelve,

so, on to twenty, I may so delve.

(21)

To Hickory for Mom's radiation treatments,

a task that receives no personal inducements.

Everyday, Monday through Friday, for seven weeks,

she makes this 60-mile trek,

driving carefully to avoid a wreck.

Now, half-way through her ordeal,

not long before the celebratory meal.

(22)

Terpsichorianism is a skill one might like to develop,

and a sense of pride might be set up.

A little practice could, if one spends a little practice

to learn more than one step,

one could actually become adept.

It is dancing,

and not just prancing.

(23)

Here I am at Granite Falls,

walking up and down its hallowed halls.

Eighth-grade classes I must teach,

and make an impression, I do so impeach.

Students study and study,

but, still some material is kind of muddy.

(24)

An assembly in the gym brings all students together,

to hear a former athlete

tell a story, that one could repeat.

His career early on was one of success,

drugs led a lot of duress.

He turned his life around,

and now has a message that will astound.

(25)

A course in Carpentry,

would be good for an unskilled person like me.

I'd learn to saw and measure,

a talent that I should treasure.

A project I would be able to complete,

and, to me, that would be quite a treat.

(26)

Entered Big Lots to buy a large-digit clock.

As I went in, I had a mental block.

I noticed that all that merchandise did not
help at all,

to do anything to jog my recall.

I bought a radio antenna for better reception,

But, it did not help my recollection.

(27)

Went to pick up two barbecue sandwiches to go,

these make my salivary glands glow.

Just as Pavlov's dogs began to salivate,

These bbq's will help my hunger abate.

Since they are so good to taste,

one can be sure that there will be no waste.

(28)

The Bible says it is more blessed to give than receive.

This is an adage of which I can believe.

The Church provides services for all of us,

if we only take advantage of thus.

Each Sunday we strive to meet,

and all our fellow parishioners are there to greet.

(29)

I went to the Catholic Church Bazaar,
it is the best I have been to so far.
So many people, I couldn't park my car,
But, the van provided, was up to par.
The food was great,
now my hunger will begin to slate.

(30)

At church, we take communion,
which gives our faith a weekly reunion.
We partake of the bread and wine,
which makes our faithful hearts feel fine.
This weekly ritual we anxiously await,
A better person than we were of late.

(31)

The waiting room at the hospital is very quiet,

and I sit around contemplating the morning's diet.

No breakfast until Mom's radiation is done,

then off to McDonald's in a run.

The daily routine is thus now done,

now off to home in a westward ride which

avoids the sun.

(32)

Veteran's Day is a very special day,

to honor those who served their country in harm's way.

If asked to serve again,

they would do so with no chagrin.

We will honor those who have served with pride,

because they protect us as they will not an

unfriendly invasion abide.

(33)

Crossword puzzles are sometimes quite an enigma,

causing me a bit of mental stigma.

Clues are given,

my mind is driven.

The solution is nigh,

it bothers me and I don't know why.

(34)

Fish tanks are interesting to observe,

fish leisurely swimming, dodging each other

with a last-second swerve.

Though fish do not have to participate

in a meaningful endeavor,

just float and eat,

and every day just repeat.

It might be boring for us,

but a lesson in leisurely living might be thus.

(35)

Basketball practice is fun,

the kids get to shoot the ball and run.

First practice deals with basic skills,

so, there is not a lot of thrills.

Competitive games will soon begin,

and the team's coach and parents will

hope they win.

(36)

Passing, dribbling, shooting are fundamentals

beginners need to learn,

If to be a good player they desire to yearn.

Lots of practice, somewhat less fun,

particularly when all they want to do is play and run.

Discipline is important for the team,

without it, they gain no victorious esteem.

(37)

P.E. classes are fun for me,

watching students frolic with glee.

Bouncing balls, shooting hoops, hitting volleyball

make good activities for all.

Each school day, for an hour and a half, they play,

and, look forward to another day.

(38)

Basketballs, volleyballs, soccer balls are

nicely round,

makes them easy to bounce up and down.

A football being oval is fun to toss around in the
gym,

but, bouncing it up and down is pretty slim.

A baseball is round and solid and will roll,

but, being hard, a hit in the head with it will

take it's toll.

(39)

The fireplace placidly sits there waiting to be lit,

if not, it will continue to idly sit.

Summer and Spring it is there,

it's usefulness one is unaware.

In winter, the ambiance and heat it

produces,

reminds one of its uses.

(40)

Joan of Arc was the video for the day

in a French class.

It was animated and interesting to watch

and so, the time did rapidly pass.

A Heroine to the French people

they came to believe,

and a place in history she did achieve.

In many heroic deeds did she participate,

only to end in a tragic fate.

(41)

It is nice to get to go to lunch,

a lot of goodies I get to munch.

Sometimes I eat to excess,

of which my middle girth is beginning

to attest.

Oh well, tomorrow is another day,

and perhaps my lunch I will delay.

(42)

To what lengths can we aspire.

Practice, study, all are needed,

so that our skills are deeply seeded.

Onward, onward, we attempt,

and never an effort do we exempt.

(43)

Almost didn't pen a poem today,
excuses abound to cause the delay.
Piddling around in the garage most of
the time,
doing things that would not rhyme.
It would be nice to miss a day,
but my goals would be set in disarray.

(44)

Each Sunday in church we kneel and pray
of course many of us do this every day.
We pray for forgiveness for every sin,
and make conscientious effort to not
digress again.
We venture out into another week,
a better life is what we seek.

(45)

Deacons make an appeal for financial support
of the church.

Into our purses we must search.

Difficult for some, easy for others.

As they look to finances to help their
churchly brothers.

Whatever they give, they probably will
not miss,

Another purchase with these funds,

would not bring to us the same amount of bliss.

(46)

From the hymnals the songs we joyously sing,

a sense of elation we hope to bring.

Four songs each service

we usually submit

in between a sermon of which we attentively sit.

To hear the Good Word holds us dear,

with the knowledge that the Holy Spirit is always
near.

(47)

Of communion on Sundays we partake,

as a remembrance of Christ's death for our sake.

Bread for the body, wine for the blood is ingested

as His memory is manifested.

A good feeling follows each trip to the alter,

and all evil thoughts are put asunder.

(48)

The Gideons throughout the world distribute Bibles

to be placed here and there.

The message of the Lord to hopefully share.

Each Gideon gives his all and it makes them

feel shamelessly tall.

To share good tidings they do endeavor,

in hope that their efforts will cause the

recipients bad deeds to sever.

(49)

Wilson, a grandson, likes to climb a tree,

he has to watch out or he will get stung by a bee.

Out on a limb he sometimes goes,

without fear he has to often grip with his toes.

Higher and higher he will ascend,

and hopefully a broken limb will not cause

him to speedily descend.

(50)

Michael, a grandson, is cool

he likes to get in the swimming pool.

He likes to swim here and there,

and doesn't seem to have a care.

Off the board, he likes to dive,

and into the water he will arrive.

(51)

Sitting around reading a book,
not even to TV do I take a look.
Most of the books I read are old,
but not so aged as to gather mold.
It's not just knowledge that I seek,
but to look into another era do I peek.

(52)

Over 700 books I have acquired,
and I say this not to be admired.
I read them and record them in
a notebook
so that into duplicate into I do not
perchance a look.
What to do with them once I am through?
I could pass, I guess, them on to you.

(53)

Gee, manini! I have passed over the hump.
To write 50 poems is quite a jump.
The goal is 100, so at 52, over half-way there.
This keeps my mindset constantly aware.
So 48 to go,
when I finish I will surely let you know.

(54)

 A grilled cheese sandwich from Allison's,
my wife did imbibe.
A sense of satisfaction did she derive.
With radiation treatments, her taste buds
are on the blink,
So finding tasty foods makes her
have to really think.
The doctor says to eat foods that are
really bland,
and I am telling you that's not so grand.

(55)

To write a poem may be a gift
I know personally I get quite a lift.
A word that rhymes
takes a lot of thought at times.
A given line ditty is my goal,
and that's easy when I am on a roll.

(56)

There came a knock at the door,
"Who is it?" I so meekly implore.
It was a lady selling a policy for cancer.
It's a little late,
I had to answer.
I wish a year or so ago I had bought one
because it would have saved me a lot of "mon."

(57)

A fan keeps me cool
that is, as a rule.
Now it is cool outside
so my fan will be set aside.
When it is hot again
I will joyfully watch its cool-
emitting spin.

(58)

Time to change oil in the car
it seems we have driven it too far.
A few quarts and a filter will do the trick,
to make the engine run pretty slick.
Five thousand miles will go by pretty fast,
too bad that oil changes just don't last.

(59)

To town to attend a party covered dish,

which we all agree will be pretty delish.

The State Chairman came to talk

party loyalty he strived to hawk.

All charged up we did depart

with new and important information to impart.

(60)

I thought the chances were pretty remote

that I would take a needle and thread to

patch a leather coat.

A year ago I did trip,

and on the side occurred a massive rip.

I would not wear it because of my vanity ego,

but now it is sewn and I am good to go.

(61)

If ever there was something I have come
to dread,

it's trying into a needle to put the thread.

Over and over I try

but it seems my dexterity will not comply.

After numerous attempts I achieve success

and to this I say, "God Bless."

(62)

Lots of pictures to hang on the wall,

even up and down the hall.

Some are old, and some are new,

but, boy, I seem to have a slew.

Looks like I need some more wall,

I wish my ceiling were a bit more tall.

(63)

Matching socks used to give me a
lot of hard knocks.
So now I pin the blues together with
a safety pin
and they don't get mixed with the blacks again.
Separate drawers for black, blue, and brown,
makes it so easy in the mornings, it will astound.

(64)

My growling stomach is reminding me it is time
for lunch.
So off I go to find something to munch.
Will it be Mexican, Japanese, or American fare,
alas, when I am hungry I don't really care.
Normally I will clean my plate,
and,in the process my hunger will slate.

(65)

Oh, my! A rainy day

so in the house I aim to stay.

The rain is in a drizzle,

and for breakfast I can hear the bacon sizzle.

But,outside I must go,

so my flashy new golf umbrella I will bestow.

(66)

In a class we watched a movie,

which was kind of groovy.

At home, on Netflix, I get to select what I desire,

elsewhere I don't know what will transpire.

A DVD or from my computer streaming,

increases my options for entertainment leaning.

(67)

Breakfast today at Abele's for the buffet,

I ate so much, you'd think it could last all day.

But alas about one o'clock the pangs will begin,

much to my chagrin.

I sure got my money's worth,

even though I have enhanced my girth.

(68)

At Abele's Restaurant memorabilia hangs from

the ceiling and on the walls and

occasionally an antique toy

is placed there for one to enjoy.

Several quotations are placed here and there,

to make us think and be aware.

It's nice to stop and eat,

a process which we will undoubtedly repeat.

(69)

Each day I strive to write a new couplet,

to make a rhyme with every other line

rhyming each time.

After a deliberation over a certain word to fit,

it comes to me like a light bulb suddenly lit.

Six lines are my max,

so that my mind I don't over tax.

(70)

In an art class, it takes a lot of appreciation

as well as a lot of imagination.

Shapes and colors one must transfix,

to get the optimum visual mix.

With clay one must shape and mold,

to make an object for one to behold.

(71)

Listening to "oldies" on the radio,

makes my memory lane begin to glow.

They stand the test of time,

and many of them actually rhyme.

Though heard repeatedly,

they never grow old for me.

(72)

Smokey, the family pooch, loves

to ride in the car.

Doesn't matter if it is near or far.

He's gone as far as Atlanta and back,

but does not seem to comfort lack.

Just mention the word "ride,"

and he goes bounding right to the auto's side.

(73)

Purrlee-May is my cat,

pretty cool to have a name like that.

Lies around and sleeps most days away,

Instead of looking for a mouse of which

to play.

Now into my lap she will lay,

and, if I keep petting her there she will stay.

(74)

I just finished my number eleven,

the Turkey Trot 5k footrace,

and, even though I am not in really

good shape, I finished at a pretty good pace.

The first-place prize was a little rubber turkey,

to beat two others, was pretty quirky.

The race was for Breast Cancer Awareness and

a Senior Project for a young lady whom I didn't

get her name,

I wish I had so I could give her some fleeting

Facebook fame.

(75)

My son is off to play golf today,

fortunately it's not too far away.

I used to play golf a lot,

I was so bad I'm glad I forgot.

It's nice now to watch others play,

and maybe I will try again some day.

(76)

A couple of years ago,

my son wrote a song a day for 365 days.

Needless to say, he had to change his

TV watching ways.

Besides the words he recorded each song.

But, having good equipment, it didn't take long.

Guitar, harmonica, and drums were played with zest,

the piano though was more of a test.

(77)

Shopping for shoes,

gives me the blues.

To get a proper fit,

gets me in a snit.

So many styles from which to choose,

makes me recall my earlier blues.

(78)

Men's shoes are much easier for me to

make a choice,

as there are only a few types on

my desirous invoice.

When I select a size 10,

my feet slide right in.

I usually wear them completely out,

even if they are built pretty stout.

(79)

A nursery rhyme has stood the test of time,

so cleverly written they did acquire,

an attribute I would yearn to aspire.

Ages and ages they have survived

and often repeated.

While modern poems are seldom heeded.

(80)

Each Sunday the lector reads two selected

verses for us to ponder.

Often, they fill us with awe and wonder.

A Baptismal service was given today,

so a new member of our flock will join the fray.

All praise given with pride.

In hope that all our sins will be set aside.

(81)

Into Aldi's to get some slaw for lunch,
adding to the other stuff to munch.
Warm apple cider was mighty tasty,
so good I didn't want to drink it too hasty.
The open oven door expelled some heat,
on this chilly day it felt mighty neat.

(82)

Suduku puzzles sometimes are not too bad,
but the five-star ones make me sad.
The choices will come down to two in different
blocks to make,
and, guess wrong most of the time I take.
Every five days an easy one will pop up,
and my spirits will nicely erupt.

(83)

What to do when one is called to substitute teach?

Are there students whom one can academically reach?

We hope they are in school to learn,

as that is what teachers yearn.

Every day teachers some knowledge impart,

with the goal that in the students' craniums

that knowledge will remain when they depart.

(84)

It's nice to sit and read,

yes it is a pleasure indeed.

So many books are there to peruse,

but only one can a person choose.

A work of fiction

often fits my predilection.

(85)

Wilson is drawing a comic book,

and Michael is taking a look.

With his left hand he makes the frames,

In which to put the refrains.

A story he will tell

and a super hero will look super swell.

(86)

For Thanksgiving I ate too much turkey

so, I am not feeling too perky.

Deviled eggs, dressing and such,

was just a little too much.

Much to my chagrin

I blew my chance to become more thin.

(87)

With pumpkin pie an hour after turkey,

with whipped cream on top,

I know now my appetite will drop.

It was so tasty

I probably ate it a trifle too hasty.

But of course later in the day,

Another slice will come into play.

(88)

I have to climb a ladder

but nothing makes me sadder.

I scale to the top hoping my hammer,

I will not drop.

Now to find a nail

Into the wall the nail I will impale.

(89)

By Wilson Cates, age 7

Captain Underpants is pretty cool,

he likes to fly,

and order pie.

He knows how to fly,

and how to jump real high.

(90)

Oh what a chore,

having to paint a rental house floor.

The walls and baseboards are next,

which makes my demeanor be vexed.

Soon it will be through,

I'm glad I don't have to paint the outside, too.

(91)

It seems that I am in need of a toothily crown,

all that chewing I have done is

wearing that tooth down.

75 years is a lot of time to gnaw

so of course it's had time to develop a flaw.

After the crown in installed today,

I will cheerfully chew away for many a day.

(92)

Entering the World of Work

is the name of a book,

upon entering a class, I took a look.

Each chapter had terms highlighted in black,

to make it easier for students' minds to attack.

Students learn the basics to get a job

and earn some cash,

and hopefully won't spend it on something rash.

(93)

In the Hickory High school cafeteria

I ate lunch

If there was a buffet I would have eaten a bunch.

The chicken sandwich I had was pretty tasty,

though as usual I ate it a little hasty.

Pineapple for dessert and iced tea

completed the fare,

I could have gotten more but, I didn't dare.

(94)

When I came home today and opened the door

to a horrific smell.

What it is, it's hard to tell.

Could it be a dead animal that was dragged

in by our cat,

but alas a look around eliminated that.

So on we search, so far in vain,

hopefully, to find it soon or we will go insane.

(95)

Another rainy day,

what can I say.

Farmers say it's too wet to plow,

but, for me I don't know how.

In the house I will stay

and with the computer I will play.

(96)

Billboards along the highways

for all to see

extolling a company's wares to

entice you and me.

Some are attractive and well done,

some are bland.

But, good or bad, there they stand.

(97)

A spacious field lies awaiting to be used.

For houses, crops, foliage, or weeds,

are yet to be infused.

Wild animals, meanwhile, feed, cavort

and play

each and every day.

Time will tell what will befall,

and that vacant spot may eventually

benefit us all.

(98)

Mixing veggies and fruits in the blender,

supposed to help us get more slender.

Round and round the blades they crush,

to make a nice delectable mush.

If we did this at least once a day,

our desired weight would probably stay.

(99)

Wood sure is versatile stuff,

It can be shaped after being very rough.

Houses, furniture, artwork -- you name it,

it covers quite a gambit.

It's fun to take plain log,

whip it into a shape we may desire,

and use the scraps to make a fire.

(100)

At last I have reached one hundred,

six-line poems that are put on paper.

A task which was quite a caper.

I thought it would take a long time,

having to dream up subjects with which to rhyme.

It was done in about a month,

and was a lot of fun.

But holy mackerel I am done!

(101)
Woops! I thought I was through,
but realizing how thin the book
would be I began to rethink anew.
So on to one hundred-ten I will surge,
and write another one when I get the urge.
Nine more shouldn't be too tough,
as this old world is full of interesting stuff.

(102)
Christmas trees so light and bright
creating such a pleasing sight.
All those baubles accumulated year after year,
sometimes makes one evoke a tear.
Every year the tradition continues to be,
so that all the family can gather together to see.

(103)

Students awaiting the next class to begin,
it may be science, English, math that they enter in.
Fresh from P.E. and the morning exercise,
now, on to academics,
to make them wise.
Some of the students apply themselves to
their advantage,
the rest will find it tougher to
academically and economically manage.

(104)

Weight training class stresses repetition,
the students lift weights from each position.
Bulking up and building strength is the goal,
but sometimes sore muscles take their toll.
All the equipment is available for them to use,
and it's so durable, it's difficult to abuse.

(105)

Leaves, leaves, everywhere, they fall

so fast I could only stare.

But now the trees are bare.

Out comes the blower and the rake

for the chore,

which taxes my weak back once more.

Bag them up, and carry them away,

too bad I can't just let them stay.

(106)

People line the streets for the Christmas Parade

of which to view.

Children, parents, and grandfolks too.

High school bands, floats and marchers go by,

drawing from the spectators a contented sigh.

Lots of waving, lots of smiles during this event,

makes the time put in by the participants well spent.

(107)

An Art class stresses imagination which, of course,
takes a certain amount of concentration.
Students draw circles, lines and such
adding water color, acrylics, or oil paints,
completes the touch.
Some students knead their clay,
which really incites their creative way.

(108)

In class, we were reading the book,
Things Fall Apart.
I wonder what knowledge it will impart.
So we began reading each of us a
line or two,
and eventually we got through.
Coming up next another book,
into which we will take a look.

(109)

I like to eat pumpkin or apple pie,

so if I don't get a bite my taste buds I will deny.

It could probably make me fat,

so what about that?

The crust is good too,

and would also be tasty for you.

(110)

Ten poems ago my goal was 100,

but rethinking again I decided to go to 110.

Now to decide on the proper format,

and luckily I found someone who will do that.

Next to put them in a book,

and hopefully some folks will take a look.

(111)

Winter weather makes me go brrrrr.

Unfortunately sometimes the sniffles will occur.

I hustle to get inside,

to make the chills subside.

Now safe and warm within,

I may not go out again.

(112)

In school they are studying: "the web of life,"

which hopefully will not cause their brains much strife.

Each species has its role to play,

if, on this earth, it wants to stay.

All will live and its life span will ply,

but, eventually all will die.

(113)

Tossing items through the air,

"Don't do it!" the substitute teacher did declare.

If you do, it won't be good,

off to the Principal's office to be sent you could.

The Principal won't like it any,

because he has to see so many.

(114)

What is love?

Is it a gift from above?

To many it will flourish,

to others broken hearts they will nourish.

To you, I hope love will stay,

for many, many a day.

(115)

What can one do when it rains pretty hard
outside.

I know all that yard work will remain unapplied.

It's best not to sit around and fret,

at least you are not getting all soggy and wet.

Best to remain inside,

and of future projects, you can decide.

(116)

An invitation to display my artwork

was recently given,

so my ego was once more driven.

On display ten of my works hung,

while in the background,

Christmas carols were sung.

A few compliments came my way,

which makes me want to display again

another day.

(117)
I have a buddy whose name is Mac.
He will always be there to cover your back.
He is often tough, and cuts no slack,
even though compassion he does not lack.
He is a good friend to have these days,
of course friendship needs to go both ways.

(118)
Sandy Beach Shag Club is a fun club to
socialize and dance.
Meeting new friends is happenstance.
A party is held every month to enjoy,
and some new dance steps we may employ.
In between our dances, other places to go we seek,
to meet new folks and not be meek.

(119)

When I attempt to tell a joke,

a giggle or two I try to evoke.

Sometimes they are funny and folks laugh,

others are corny and I have made a gaff.

Onward, I will continue with these mirthful forays,

to spread some cheer into a recipient's todays.

(120)

Finally made it to the end,

120 couplets did I append.

To a publisher I will now unfold,

the printed copy I will behold.

Daily experiences have been

obviously alluded to,

in hopes that some humor

will be given to you.

(121)

Students at lunch in the cafeteria,

their noise levels close to hysteria.

Talking to their tablemates is obviously

not in style,

so they must persist in talking across the isle.

Silent lunch they were threatened to get,

if they continue their loudness bit.

(122)

5:30, 6:00, 6:30 are times that can be a real rub,

those times are when I usually get a call to sub.

If nary a call comes in,

I begin to snooze again.

Often I refuse the job request,

thus I continue with my rest.

(123)

Lots of hammering and scraping
on my roof undo,
to be nicely replaced anew.
Several leaks had transpired,
placing buckets around the house
made me tired.
With the new roof, we will be
dryly snug,
for which I will give the roofer,
my son, a great big hug.

(124)

With close to 3,500 friends on Facebook,
I am never at a loss for a place to look.
Every day for the past three years,
I have sent out birthday greetings to
my Facebook peers.
Many of them I know, some I don't
know at all,
but a nice birthday recognition does not appall.
I will continue this for quite a spell,
unless something happens and I become unwell.

(125)

Land sakes, alive!
125 poems did I derive.
I thought maybe 100, 120, were it,
but seems that a poetic fever I did beget.
I could probably go on and on like this,
but my readers might give me a groanful dis.
Maybe this one will be the last one,
even though penning them is a lot of fun.

(126)

Off to the dentist office I went,
I hope it was time well spent.
"Open wide," he says to me,
better to take a look, you see.
A crown is what I need,
so for the next ten days,
on the right side I must knead.

(127)

To Oak Hill Elementary School
Christmas program did we go to observe.
Each class did a song, and did move and swerve.
Students sprawled all across the gym floor,
awaiting what was to be in store.
From kindergarten to grade five they
sat in groups at attention,
standing only to sing the selection
which the director will mention.

(128)

Another small windfall came my way today,
Instead of irrationally spending,
a few bills I will defray.
It would be nice if it happened more often,
so my checking account will soften.
But I don't anticipate these with much hope,
otherwise, I would go around and mope.

(129)

When things are bad and you feel blue.

A prayer or two might just pull you through.

Look around for a friend to talk to,

it might just be what you need to pull you through.

People fret and I do too,

But, somehow, somewhere, something will pull
you through.

(130)

At T.G.I. Friday's in Asheville to await a

friend to enter the room.

A couple of lagers, I will consume.

Ten TV screens depict several sports to see,

but, it's basketball for me.

Not many folks in the bar at three,

which is ok because it's off to see

Delbert McClinton in concert for me.

(131)

The crew sets up, and the band gets ready
to play.
The leader of the band, says: "Guy's,
everything looks ok."
Eagerly awaiting the soulful rendering of
a particular song,
so that they can sing along.
All at once the band begins,
watching below the stage to see their fans grin.

(132)

Let's go to the game
funny from a distance all the players look the
same
Some folks have their favorite players they have
come to see,
and that sometimes applies to me.
Good competition and sportsmanship is
in the coach's game plan of action,
hoping for a favorable fan reaction.

(133)

To Hickory we went to shop and spend,
and thus my checking account, it will upend.
To O'Charley's to enjoy their fare,
it could not be better elsewhere,
we do declare.
Back to Morganton we will go,
but not too rapidly
because the traffic is slow.

(134)

The Advent of Lessons and Carols
was the program for church today.
Each lesson and carol reminded us
of our need to pray.
Nine readers did proclaim,
the most wondrousness of His name.
The hymns were sung with vigor by all,
and as we exit we hope that a better
life will befall.

(135)

When I dance I feel like I could go all night,
but, if I did my muscles sure would ache a mite.
Maybe it's the music that motivates my moves,
and sets me onto my various grooves.
Mostly oldies do I hear,
besides dancing to them,
I am reminded of yesteryear.

(136)

The purpose of this little ditty is
to make no cents.
In England, I would be using pounds and pence.
It's nice just to sit and pose,
and hope that a thought will a "rose."
Usually, it doesn't take long for something to tick,
which, I think, is pretty slick.

(137)

All these verses of poetic punning,

but nothing have I written

about my running.

For thirty-three years in 5k races,

I have joined others with my paces.

Lots of trophies and ribbons did I win,

and hopefully next year I can do it again.

(138)

My jukebox has 50 45's,

and plays 100 tunes, mostly oldies.

After owning it for over 25 years,

I am glad they are not moldies.

At Christmas time the Platters ring forth

their rendition of "White Christmas" many,

many times each day.

Over and over, it will play.

Fats Domino, the Platters, the Coasters,

the Drifters, and many others are there.

Push a couple of buttons and the

melodious sounds begin to blare.

(139)

I can't think of a better time of the year,

when families gather to share Christmas cheer.

Presents are shared with one another,

to show that we love both sister and brother.

Gathering at least once a year,

which makes the season

to be held so dear.

(140)

Lordy, lordy, this is number one-forty to me,

not by age, of course, as depicted in

these poems, you see.

But they are mainly poems of things,

happening to me.

On and on, I strive to concoct a rhyme,

painstakingly constructed one at a time.

Some are pretty good, others not so hot,

but alas they were designed without

a central plot.

(141)

Wilson is reveling at his new toys,
which usually happens
at Christmas time for boys.
Opening each one for inspection,
not a detail escapes his detection.
Many hours of fun will have he,
as he plays with each one with glee.

(142)

We would like to note that Bryan, our son,
now has a new coat.
It should keep him warm and snug,
so Stephanie, his wife, will be sure
to give him a great big hug.
It looks like it is made to last,
if it doesn't we will be aghast.

(143)

Michael got, we think, what he wanted to get.

If he didn't, he is such a young gentleman

he would not pitch a fit.

His favorites he will select,

and the others he will collect.

Gifts now for Christmas he got,

and on January 12 his birthday,

he will still get a lot.

(144)

We had fun selecting Stephanie's coat,

and we could have added a hat,

but we didn't think about that.

If it is not the style or color

she would adopt,

our feelings won't be hurt if

the coat is swapped.

If so off to Old Navy she will go,

to pick out one she can wear--

as her chilly cheeks begin to glow.

(145)

Christopher, my son, will be aglow
as he watches the Medieval Show.
The dinner show is quite a treat,
as the actors perform on horseback
many a feat.
It's a chance to glance back
to a time in the past,
and provide a memory that
will for a long-time last.

(146)

Adair, our daughter-in-law, at
Christmas time will receive
many a gift.
These of course will give her
quite a lift.
She will open them always
with a smile,
and be cheerful all the while.
Thanking each and every one,
she will enter in with
the family fun.

(147)

What can you get your bride,

when for 52 years has been by your side.

In the past, she got a Rolex

which will last and last.

This year I fear,

will be a lot leaner my dear.

(148)

And--what about me?

Do I get stuff that to me is actually free?

Will I be happy as a dad?

You can bet I will be very glad.

On to next year we eagerly await,

to see if Santa is at our hearth's grate.

(149)

Give me an inch, and I will take a mile.

Give me a gift, and I'll give you a smile.

Help me if I am in trouble,

and I will return the favor, except double.

Give a compliment

and I will from some sinful deed repent.

(150)

I suppose it is pretty nifty,

that I have composed 150.

At first I wanted to have two

poems to a page and sixty pages,

but new ones came to me in different stages.

At 150 I will quit,

and try to let my noodle rest a bit.

(151)

I was going to quit at 150, but on a visit,

I hastily scripted a poem about their

young lass who was there.

Ok I said, I will enter it along with

the others with care.

Please do, the mother plead, so we may

take a look, when we see

it in your book.

(152)

Nora is a sweet little girl,

when she dances,

she does quite a twirl.

She's a cute little blond,

of which later on,

all the boys are going to be fond.

She is growing like a weed you see

so it will be a beautiful young lady she will be.

(153)

I wonder what good it does to collect
small gas pumps and other memorabilia,
except to enjoy and collect dust.
But I guess the plastic ones won't rust.
Small cars I also amass in quite a number,
so my shelving they do encumber.
My collection of over 700 pre-1948 books
is another hobby for me to do.
After reading them, I could sell them
or pass them on to you.

(154)

This one was written in haste,
in the urgency to fill in space.
Two poems to a page makes
this one necessary in this case.
Now it's all even at two to a page,
not that one to a page will enrage.
But 154 tidily evens it up for the book,
and 72 pages of poems can be betook.

Jim Cates, Ed.D

A.A. -- Business Administration, Campbell College,

B.S. -- Business Education, Appalachian State Teachers College

M.A. -- Business Education, Appalachian State Teachers College

Ed.S. -- Community College Teaching, Appalachian State Teachers College

Ed.D -- Higher Education & Teaching, Nova Southeastern University

Two-year diploma -- Auto Mechanics, McDowell Technical College

Further graduate studies:

Economics & Vocational Education, UNC--Chapel Hill

School Administration Certification--Western Carolina University

Office Management--Memphis State University

Secretarial Education--Georgia Tech

Author: Money-ish Stuff--soon to be published.

Avid Reader, Shagger, collector (books, vintage cars, small-toy cars, beer cans, small gas pumps, lunch boxes), runner, found-object artist,

    Poet? Author?

Proud to be a non-television viewer for over six years

Never smoked--proud of that, too.

Married, 52 years, two sons.

The onset of these little ditties began while trying to overcome boredom while receiving chemotherapy for the first time on an outpatient bed for seven hours. Having already completed two cross-word puzzles, two suduku's, checked Facebook, sent out birthday greetings, and read email, I was at a loss as to fill out the remaining time.

So, I decided to compose a brief poem of six lines to explain my journey to combat Follicular Lymphoma. This activity, I continued for all six trips to the doctor's office, and dutifully, recorded them on Facebook. As it were, I was pleasantly encouraged by the many statements received of support, as well as prayers, for my plight.

Then, one day I penned another short poem (couplet) based on some inconsequential event. So, on to twenty I went. Then 50, then 100, 125, 140 and finally 154

Upon recommendation from a friend, I contacted a person who does the formatting, who also recommended a printer, and thus, the small book: 154 Cates Poetic "Jim's."

Thanks for reading 154 Cates Poetic "Jims"

www.ingramcontent.com/pod-product-compliance
Lightning Source LLC
Chambersburg PA
CBHW061501040426
42450CB00008B/1449